Maui

IMAGES OF THE VALLEY ISLAND

Photography by
Douglas Peebles

Mutual Publishing

Library of Congress Catalog Card Number: 2003107829

ISBN-10: 1-56647-602-X
ISBN-13: 978-1-56647-602-7

First Printing, November 2003
Second Printing, May 2004
Third Printing, November 2004
Fourth Printing, July 2005
Fifth Printing, April 2006
Sixth Printing, June 2007

Mutual Publishing, LLC
1215 Center Street, Suite 210
Honolulu, Hawai'i 96816
Ph: (808) 732-1709 Fax: (808) 734-4094
email: info@mutualpublishing.com
www.mutualpublishing.com

Printed in China

Lahaina

Ke'anae Peninsula

Sugar cane fields, Central Valley

'Jaws', Hāna Coast

Molokini Island

Whale watching

Oneloa Beach (Big Beach, Mākena)

Lahaina Harbor

Sunrise, Haleakalā

Haleakalā National Park

Silversword, Haleakalā National Park

Haleakalā National Park

Kanahā Beach

Olowalu, West Maui Mountains

'Oheʻo Gulch, Seven Sacred Pools, Kīpahulu, Hāna Coast

Road to Hāna

Kapalua

Hāna

Hula hālau, Wai'ānapanapa

Kāʻanapali

Kitesurfing, Hoʻokipa

Windsurfing, Hoʻokipa

Orchid farm, West Maui Mountains

Hāna

'Ulupalakua Ranch, Upcountry Maui

Olinda, Upcountry Maui

Kāʻanapali Beach

WaiLea

Pā'ia

La Pérouse Bay

Whale watching, Lahaina

Kaupō

Kahakuloa

ʻĪao Valley

Road to Haleakalā

Manawainui Valley

Sunrise, Haleakalā

Kapalua

Oneloa Beach (Big Beach, Mākena)

Ke'anae Peninsula, Hāna

Mākena, with a view of Molokini and Kahoʻolawe

Pi'ilanihale Heiau, Hāna Coast